Pet Projects

Hip HAMSTER Projects

Loads of cool craft projects inside

Isabel Thomas

raintree
a Capstone company — publishers for children

Raintree is an imprint of Capstone Global Library Limited, a company incorporated in England and Wales having its registered office at 7 Pilgrim Street, London, EC4V 6LB – Registered company number: 6695582

www.raintree.co.uk
myorders@raintree.co.uk

Edited by Helen Cox Cannons and Holly Beaumont
Designed by Philippa Jenkins
Picture research by Tracy Cummins
Production by Helen McCreath
Originated by Capstone Global Library Ltd
Printed and bound in China

ISBN 978 1 406 29823 9
19 18 17 16 15
10 9 8 7 6 5 4 3 2 1

British Library Cataloguing in Publication Data
A full catalogue record for this book is available from the British Library.

Acknowledgements
We would like to thank the following for permission to reproduce photographs:
Alamy: imageBROKER, 12; Getty Images: Todd Sappington, Cover Bottom Left; Shutterstock: Brooke Whatnall, Design Element, Elya Vatel, 17 Bottom Right, 28 Bottom Left, George M Photography, 28 (hat), Igor Kovalchuk, 1, Multiple Use, Jagodka, 22 (hamster), SeDmi, 18 Top Left.

All other photography by Capstone Studio: Karon Dubke.

Every effort has been made to contact copyright holders of material reproduced in this book. Any omissions will be rectified in subsequent printings if notice is given to the publisher.

All the internet addresses (URLs) given in this book were valid at the time of going to press. However, due to the dynamic nature of the internet, some addresses may have changed, or sites may have changed or ceased to exist since publication. While the author and publisher regret any inconvenience this may cause readers, no responsibility for any such changes can be accepted by either the author or the publisher.

Safety instructions for adult he

Some of the projects in this boo[...] an
adult – these are indicated in the[...]

ADULT
HELP

Contents

Hung up on hamsters!.............4

Fabric crafts......................6

Get crafty with paper..........10

Hamster-rific DIY projects..12

Kitchen creations 16

Animal art 18

Upcycle!...........................22

Throw a hamster party!.......26

Hamster facts 30

Templates........................31

Index..............................32

Look out for the paw-print icons. These tell you how long each project will take.

= up to 30 minutes

= up to 1 hour

= more than 1 hour

Hung up on hamsters!

If you're hung up on hamsters, you'll love the projects in this book. If you are lucky enough to have a hamster yourself, or just love those cute cheeks, there is so much to make and do.

- �֍ Make gifts for friends or relatives
- ✦ Decorate your bedroom with hamster designs
- ✦ Create homemade hamster treats and toys
- ✦ Throw a hamster-themed party!

At the back of the book you'll find a link to a web page packed with templates to use in the projects, and tips on how to use them to create designs of your own!

Getting started

Before starting each project, read the instructions carefully and make sure you have everything you need. Find out if you will need an adult to help with any of the steps. If you are planning to reuse or recycle an object, or decorate walls, clothes or furniture, check that it's ok first.

Nibblesome notecards page 11

Pocket hamster page 6

Hamster pops page 26

Pet view

Look out for my tips on hamster care as you scamper through the book!

Working safely

Work in an area where you can make a mess, using newspaper to protect the table or floor. Make sure you open the windows or work outside if you are using paint or glue. Keep pets away while you are crafting. Never use paint or glue near a pet – the fumes can be dangerous for animals.

Things... to keep in your craft kit

- Scissors, pens, pencils, paints, paintbrush, ruler, sticky tape and PVA glue.

- Pretty found objects such as feathers, stones and buttons.

- Scraps of pretty fabric, paper, card, newspapers and magazines.

- Boxes, jars and containers with interesting shapes (wash and dry food containers before storing them).

- Sewing materials such as needle and thread, wool, yarn, ribbons and trimmings.

Fabric crafts

Sadly you can't take your hamster to school with you. But you can take these cute crafts!

Pocket hamster

Turn scraps of fabric into a portable pet, small enough to pop in your pencil case.

1 Find the pocket hamster template on the website (see page 31), print and cut it out. Pin the template on to the fabric, and cut out matching shapes in felt or furry fabric and white or cream fabric.

2 Stack the two pieces of fabric together (with the furry sides facing in). Sew around the outside of the shapes, leaving a gap at the tail end.

3 Tie off the thread and turn the shape inside out.

4 Make a funnel from card, and use it to help you fill the fabric shape with rice or beans. Stop before the hamster is full. Sew up the gap tightly.

You will need:

- tracing paper, pencil and scissors
- felt or furry fabric
- white or cream fabric
- card
- needle and thread
- uncooked rice or dried beans
- three small beads

5 Sew the beads on to make the nose and eyes. Using the project templates, cut two ears from the leftover white or cream fabric and sew them in place. Add whiskers by sewing four long loops of thread around the nose bead, and cutting through the loops.

Your fluffy friend can double as a pincushion for sewing projects!

Pet view

I like to rest and sleep during the day, so please only handle me in the evenings when I'm already awake. I don't like bright lights or loud noises.

TOP TIP

Sprinkle in some dried lavender to make a hamster that smells as lovely as it looks!

Super-soft pictures

Create a cross-stitch hamster that's as strokeable as the real thing!

1. Start by printing a photograph of your hamster on to graph paper. Alternatively, draw a hamster design on to graph paper and colour it in.

2. Secure the cross-stitch fabric in an embroidery hoop. Using a pencil, sketch the outline of your design on to it, square by square.

3. Thread the needle with a piece of wool or thread, and knot the end. Starting in one corner of the design, thread the needle up through the canvas so the knot is at the back.

4. Sew over each square with cross-stitch, using the graph paper as a guide. When you need to change colour, knot the thread at the back.

You will need:

- graph paper
- pencil or coloured pens
- cross-stitch fabric
- embroidery needle
- wool or embroidery thread in hamstery colours
- embroidery hoop or empty picture frame and drawing pins
- scissors

An embroidery needle has a large eye and rounded end.

TOP TIP

If you don't have an embroidery hoop, pinning the fabric to an empty frame will keep it flat while you sew.

Small cross-stitch pictures are perfect for displaying in a key ring or frame.

Pencil pet

Cut two ovals from felt. Glue or sew them together, leaving a 1-cm gap at the large end. Glue or sew on eyes, ears, nose and whiskers, and simply slip on to a pencil. Why not make a host of hamsters in rainbow colours?

TOP TIP

Turn your softies into key rings by sandwiching a loop of ribbon with a key ring attachment between the layers of felt.

Get crafty with paper

Uncage your creativity with these hamster-inspired projects.

Just add hamsters!

Do you ever get pretty hamster wrapping paper you can't bear to throw away? Use it to make a hamster-rific pet record book!

1 Cut or tear the magazine or wrapping paper into pieces.

2 Paint a small area of the notebook with diluted glue. Stick on pieces of the paper, overlapping the edges.

3 Repeat until you have covered the notebook with pictures. Leave to dry.

You will need:
- notebook
- old hamster magazines or wrapping paper
- scissors
- diluted PVA glue (3 parts glue to 1 part water) and brush

Stick the paper on with PVA glue. Brush over a coat of diluted glue to seal your design.

Pet view

Keeping a pet record book will help you to spot if I'm ill or injured. If my eating or sleeping habits change, take your record book along to show the vet.

Nibblesome notecards

A few folds turn a square of paper into something much cuter.

1 Fold the square of paper in half. Then, fold the left third of the rectangle across the middle third.

2 Take the bottom left corner and fold it back up to the middle. Crease firmly, and then tuck it back in on itself.

3 Next, fold the bottom corner outwards to make a paw and fold the top corner down to make an ear.

4 Finally, fold the top corner backwards to make a tail. Add an eye, nose and whiskers to finish your hamster.

Don't forget to write a secret note inside!

Hamster-rific DIY projects

It's not just you that needs privacy in a busy house. Help your hamster to hide away during the day, and make her feel safe when you handle her in the evenings.

Coconut hideaway

Coconut shells make brilliant hamster hideaways. They are just the right size to snuggle up in, and because they are both hard and natural, they are perfect for chewing on.

1 Ask an adult to saw the top off a coconut, about a quarter of the way down. Another option is to put the coconut in a plastic bag and swing it against a wall or floor to break it open. Make sure you do this outside!

2 Use a spoon to scrape the flesh out of the coconut – yum! – then rinse and dry the shell. If there are sharp edges, sand them down, then rinse and dry again.

3 Pop the coconut shell into your hamster's home, along with nesting material.

You will need:
- coconut
- spoon
- sandpaper

5 things... to do with a cardboard tube

🐹 Your hamster needs plenty to do inside its cage. Empty kitchen roll tubes make great ramps, tunnels and hidey-holes.

🐹 You hamster loves to gnaw, shred and chew. This is good for its teeth. Cardboard tubes are easy to replace when they wear down.

🐹 Hide a dry hamster treat inside a soft cardboard tube, and fold the ends down. Can your hamster work out how to get it out?

🐹 Stuff hay inside the tube and position it in the cage as a hay feeder, to stop the hay mixing with the bedding.

🐹 Try the pencil pot project on page 24.

Pet view

Wild hamsters live under ground, and never stray too far from their burrows. This is why I'm timid, and need plenty of places to hide, or snuggle into when it's time for a snooze.

Hamster lanterns

Hamsters are usually only awake in the evening and night. This means the best time to handle your hamster is in the early morning or evening, when they are already awake. The soft light from these pretty lanterns will make your hamster feel at ease and help you bond.

1 Cut or tear the tissue paper into pieces. Include one or two hamster shapes from the templates on the website (see page 31).

2 Glue the tissue paper shapes on to the outside of the jar, to make pretty patterns.

3 Paint the jar with a coat of diluted PVA glue (1 part glue to 3 parts water).

You will need:

- old jar, washed and dried, label removed
- tissue paper in different colours
- scissors
- PVA glue and brush

 TOP TIP

Light your lanterns with bike lights, glow sticks or battery-powered tea lights. Never use a candle.

Pet view

It's a bad idea to keep me in your bedroom. I'm only awake at night, so my noisy playing and exercising might stop you sleeping! Find me a spot that is quiet in the day, and where the lights go off at the same time every night.

4 When the glue is dry, your lantern is ready to use. Place a light source inside and screw on the lid.

Turn the main lights off and watch your lantern glow!

Pet pot

It's easy to transfer hamster pictures on to a jar. Just print a design, roll up the paper and pop it inside the jar. Draw or paint over it using a glass pen or paint. This makes a cute holder for a battery-powered tea light, or a pretty place to store dry hamster food.

Kitchen creations

Every hamster loves a treat, but did you know that some shop-bought treats have unhealthy ingredients, such as sugar and colourings? Make these delicious alternatives.

Hamster salad bar

Hamsters love leaves such as clover and dandelion, but it's important not to give them plants that grew near a roadside (which can be dirty) or may have been treated with chemicals (which can be poisonous). Homegrown greens are a great way to top up your hamster's daily diet safely.

1 Cover the bottom of the container with a layer of gravel. Add potting compost until the container is two-thirds full.

2 Water the compost lightly, then plant seeds following the instructions on the packet. Water the seeds, then cover the container with a layer of cling film and keep it in a warm place. Remember to keep the soil damp.

3 Once seedlings have sprouted, move the container to a sunny spot, such as a windowsill, and keep it well watered.

You will need:
- container (flowerpot)
- gravel
- potting compost
- cling film
- seeds of hamster-friendly plants (e.g. dandelion, groundsel, clover, beansprouts)

Pet view
Give me greens in small amounts to stop me hiding spare food around my home, which will soon start to rot – yuck! Some greens, such as rhubarb, potato and tomato leaves, are poisonous to hamsters, so always check with an expert first.

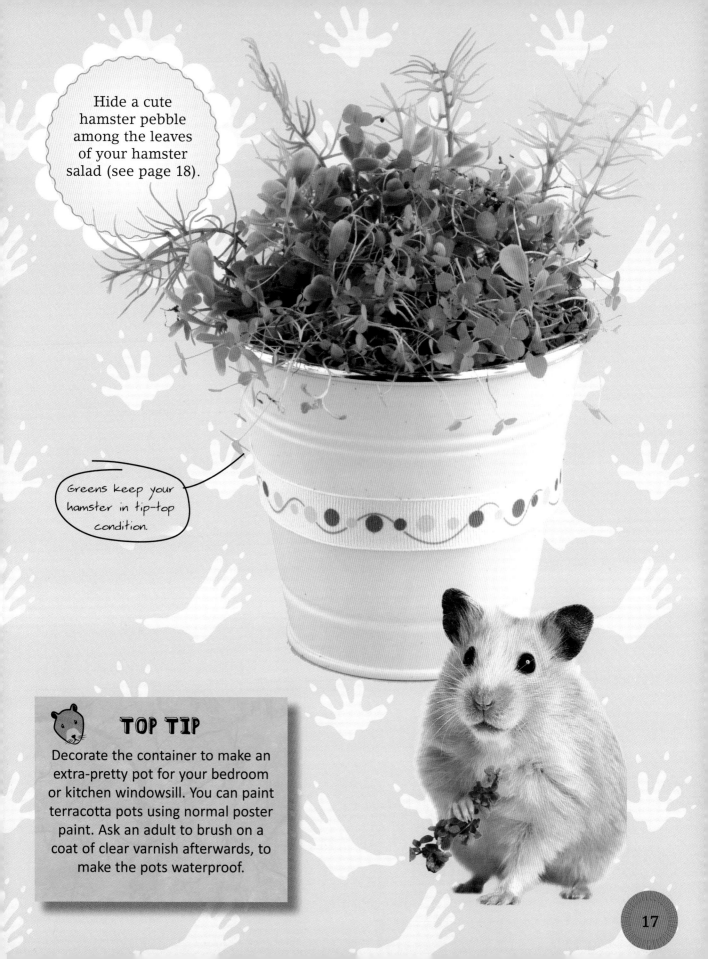

Hide a cute hamster pebble among the leaves of your hamster salad (see page 18).

Greens keep your hamster in tip-top condition.

TOP TIP

Decorate the container to make an extra-pretty pot for your bedroom or kitchen windowsill. You can paint terracotta pots using normal poster paint. Ask an adult to brush on a coat of clear varnish afterwards, to make the pots waterproof.

Animal art

Your hamster may not be able to live in your bedroom, but you can fill it with reminders of your BFF – best fluffy friend!

Perfect paperweight

Use fur-toned paint to turn a pebble into a work of art.

You will need:

- large, smooth pebble with a tapered end (the kind you'd find on a beach)
- acrylic paints
- paintbrush
- diluted PVA glue (3 parts glue to 1 part water)

1 Start by painting your pebble white. When the paint is dry to the touch, brush on tiny strokes of dark brown paint, then add strokes of lighter paint over it.

2 Paint black eyes, dabbing a tiny dot of white on to each eye to make them gleam (use the end of the brush handle to do this). Add black and pink ears, a pink nose and mouth, and whiskers in white paint.

3 When the paint is dry, carefully brush on a coat of diluted PVA glue to seal your design.

Q
Could you ever love a rock?

A
Yes, when it looks like a hamster!

Keep out!

This "keep out" sign is just too cute to argue with! Why not make one for your hamster too? Download the templates (see page 31), and print. Transfer them to a piece of sturdy card, and cut them out. Glue them back to back, and decorate each side. On one side write something like "Come back later, I'm dozing" and on the other side write "Please say hello!"

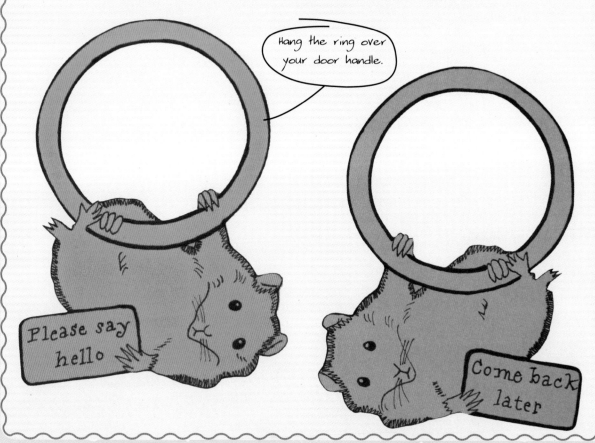

Hang the ring over your door handle.

Please say hello

Come back later

Bracelet buddy

Use salt dough to make a charming hamster charm.

1. Mix the flour and salt together, then pour in the water slowly, stirring to make a dough. Knead (squeeze and mix) the dough with your hands to make it soft, adding a few more drops of water if you spot any cracks.

2. Roll two small balls of salt dough. Pinch one ball to make the bottom wider than the top. This is your hamster's head.

3. Squish the head on to the body, so the cheeks stick out on the sides. Roll some smaller salt dough balls to add paws, ears and a belly.

4. Push two beads into the face to make eyes and another bead to make a nose.

5. Push the eye pin into the top of the hamster's head. Leave the salt dough to dry overnight.

6. When the dough is completely dry, paint your model using acrylic paint. Draw in your hamster's mouth using permanent marker pen. Add a coat of diluted PVA glue to seal your design.

You will need:

- 150 g (5 oz.) flour
- 75 g (2½ oz.) salt
- 60 ml water
- two small black beads
- eye pin (from a bead shop)
- cocktail sticks
- acrylic paints
- diluted PVA glue
- permanent marker pen

Thread your hamster charm on to a bracelet, mobile phone or pencil case.

Cheeky cartoons

You can make cute hamster cartoons using fingerprints. Dip a finger in ink, and press on to paper. Make prints in different colours. Have fun adding ears, eyes, nose, whiskers and paws. How many expressions can you give your hamsters?

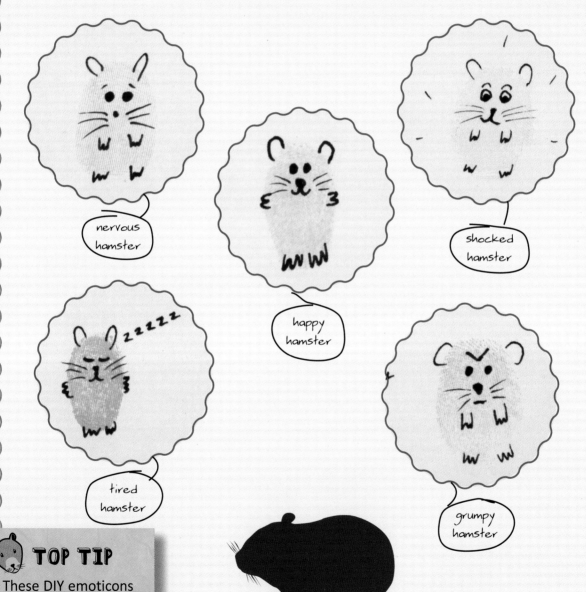

nervous hamster

happy hamster

shocked hamster

tired hamster

grumpy hamster

TOP TIP

These DIY emoticons are a quick way to personalize cards and invitations.

Upcycle!

Don't throw out old food packaging and containers. Recycle it into awesome accessories for your hamster, and help save the planet at the same time.

Make me a maze

Hamsters need plenty of exercise and they love to explore. This amazing maze will get your hamster's whiskers twitching.

You will need:

- old cardboard packaging without colours or prints
- cardboard tubes (e.g. empty kitchen roll tubes)
- natural materials such as old coconut shells
- scissors

Make sure everything is empty and clean, with no sharp edges. Remove any plastic parts.

Egg boxes make good hiding places.

1. Use a large cardboard box as a base, cutting the sides down until they are around 30 cm (12 in.) high. This will help you to wedge objects into place without using glue or tape, and will stop your hamster from escaping.

22

2 Make platforms supported by slots in the wall. Hamsters love to stop in spots like these and clean themselves.

3 Slot pieces of card together to make a maze, and join several tubes together to make long, branching tunnels. Make some holes smaller than others, so your hamster can enjoy squeezing through.

4 Cut ramps out of cardboard, and use a hard-tipped pen to score dents to help your hamster hang on. Having tiny feet has its advantages!

Hide a hamster treat inside for your really clever rodent to track down.

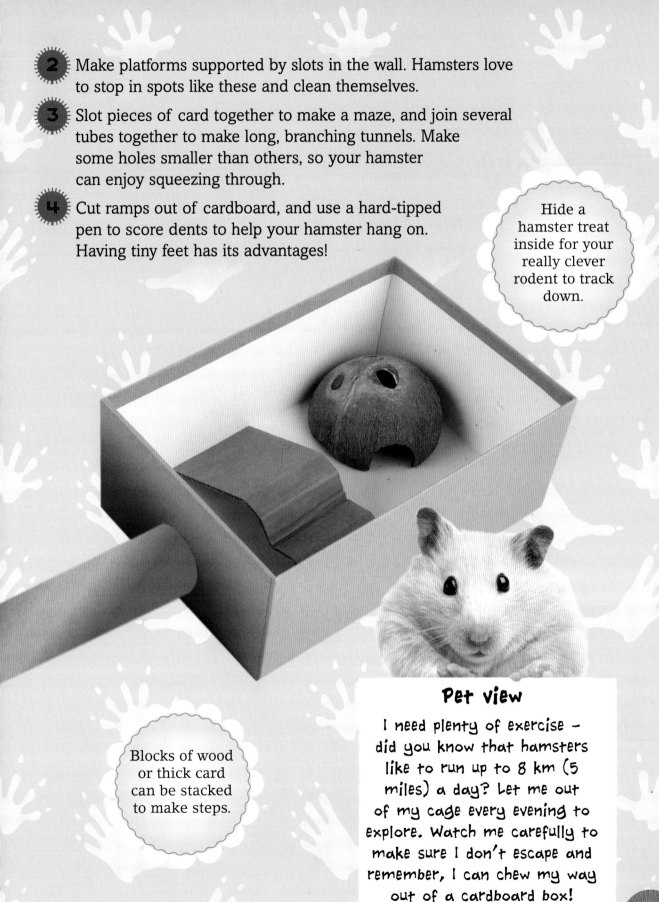

Blocks of wood or thick card can be stacked to make steps.

Pet view
I need plenty of exercise — did you know that hamsters like to run up to 8 km (5 miles) a day? Let me out of my cage every evening to explore. Watch me carefully to make sure I don't escape and remember, I can chew my way out of a cardboard box!

Pots from packaging

Hamsters can pack a lot of food into their chubby cheeks, which means lots of leftover food packaging. Transform the empty bags into woven pots, for storing your stuff in style.

1 Clean and dry the empty feed bags. Cut them up into strips 5 cm (2 in.) wide. You will need four 30-cm (12-in.) strips, and around eight 20-cm (8-in.) strips.

2 Fold each strip over on itself twice, to create stronger strips around 1 cm (½ in.) wide.

3 Cut a circle of card 5 cm (2 in.) wide. This will be the base of your pot. Stick the 30-cm (12-in.) strips across the base in a star pattern, so they are evenly spaced.

4 Turn the base over and fold the strips so they stick straight up into the air. Place an empty cardboard tube on the base, and use an elastic band to hold the strips loosely against the tube. This will be a guide for weaving your pot.

You will need:

- empty dry feed bags
- scissors
- thick cardboard
- sticky tape or strong glue
- large elastic band

5 Take one of the 20-cm (8-in.) strips and tape it to the inside of one of the upright strips. Now weave the strip around the tube, in and out of the upright strips. When you get back to the start, tape the ends of the strip together, and trim off any excess.

6 Repeat step 5 with the other 20-cm (8-in.) strips, working your way up the tube. When you are happy that your pot is high enough, remove the tube. Snip the upright strips so they finish 1 cm (½ in.) above the top of the pot. Then fold them down and glue them in place.

 TOP TIP

Give the whole pot a coat of watered down PVA glue to make it super-strong!

Throw a hamster party!

Your pet is part of the family, so celebrate his or her birthday with a party in their honour.

Hamster pops

These bite-sized cakes are super-cute and definitely super-yummy.

1 Crumble the cake into a mixing bowl to make fine crumbs. Add icing, one spoonful at a time, until the mixture sticks together like dough.

2 Break off small pieces of the dough and roll them into balls. Add two small lumps of dough to each ball to make ears. Put the balls into a fridge for an hour. Meanwhile, ask an adult to melt the white chocolate for you.

You will need:

- sponge cake
- buttercream icing
- white chocolate buttons
- wooden or rolled-paper sticks
- pink heart-shaped sprinkles
- small edible silver balls
- black writing icing or small amount of melted milk chocolate
- colander (upside down)

Pet view

Remember, cake pops are for people only! Never feed me human treats such as chocolate and cornflakes.

3 When the balls of cake are firm, take them out of the fridge. Dip each stick into the melted chocolate, and push it into the cake ball.

The chocolate will help the stick to stay in place.

4 Holding the stick, dip the ball of cake into the melted white chocolate and roll it from side to side until it is completely covered.

5 Carefully slot the stick into the colander to hold it in place.

6 While the chocolate is still wet, stick on a pink heart-shaped sprinkle to make a nose and small silver balls to make the eyes.

7 Repeat these steps until you have coated every cake ball. Put the cake pops in a cool place.

8 When the chocolate has set, use the writing icing or melted milk chocolate to add a mouth to each one.

Keep the cake pops in the fridge until you are ready to serve them.

Make a hamster piñata

A piñata is an exciting party game that is broken open to reveal the treats inside.

1 Blow up the balloons and tie the ends. Tear the newspaper into strips. Mix the glue, flour and water together to make a thin paste.

2 Dip the newspaper strips into the paste and use them to cover each balloon. Add three layers of newspaper, leaving each layer to dry before adding the next.

3 When the final layer is completely dry, pop the balloons with a pin. Carefully cut the bottom off each balloon, cutting around 5 cm (2 in.) from the ties. Tape the cut ends of the balloons together, to make a figure of eight shape.

4 Cut a small flap at the top of the piñata. This will be where you put in the treats.

You will need:

- two balloons
- 85 ml PVA glue
- 150 g (5 oz.) plain flour
- 500 ml water
- newspaper
- paintbrush
- pin and scissors
- sticky tape
- PVA glue for decorating
- crepe paper or tissue paper in brown, white, black and pink
- assorted craft papers
- string

5 Decorate your piñata with coloured tissue or crepe paper. To make fur, cut strips of paper and give each one a fringe by making small cuts into one of the long edges. Glue the strips on to the piñata so they overlap.

6 Cut out black eyes, brown ears and a pink nose. Glue them on to the face.

TOP TIP
Start from the tail and work backwards.

Pet view
Make me my own piñata, by putting some treats in a cardboard tube and folding over the ends (see page 23). I'll have fun working out how to get in. Remember not to give me anything that has been coloured, painted or glued.

Fill the piñata with treats, and hang it up using string. Take it in turns to bash the piñata until the treats fall out!

29

Hamster facts

5 facts... for hamster lovers

- Humans have kept hamsters as pets for less than 100 years, but the UK is now home to half a million pet hamsters.

- Could you sniff out your brother or sister in a crowd? Hamsters use their sense of smell to recognize their relatives.

- Hamsters can have up to ten babies at a time, and the babies can have their own babies after just six weeks!

- Like many nocturnal animals hamsters can't see very well. They explore using their whiskers instead.

- The actor Emma Watson dedicated an acting award to a pet hamster called Millie.

Find out more

Visit the RSPCA for tips on caring for pet hamsters.
www.rspca.org.uk/adviceandwelfare/pets/rodents/hamsters

Learn about hamster history at The British Hamster Association.
www.britishhamsterassociation.org.uk

The BCSPA has written a hamster care guide especially for children.
www.spca.bc.ca/assets/documents/youth/PDFs/hamster-care-guide.pdf

Templates

Visit **www.raintree.co.uk/content/download** and select
"Hip Hamster Projects" to download free templates to use with the
projects in this book. You can also use them to create your own hamster designs.
Once you have printed a template, follow these tips to transfer it to the material
you are working with.

• Use masking tape to hold a sheet of tracing or baking paper over your chosen
  design and draw over the outline with a soft pencil.

• Tape the paper on to the surface you'd like to transfer the picture to.

• Draw over the lines using a pen with a hard point.

TOP TIP

Digital templates are
easy to scale up and
down, so you can
customize the size to
suit your project.

Index

baby hamsters 30

cake pops 26–7
cardboard tubes 13, 22–23, 29
cartoons 21
coconut hideaway 12
craft kit 5
cross-stitch hamster picture 8–9

door sign 19

exercise 23

fabric crafts 6–9
fingerprinting 21
food storage jar 15

glue 5
greens 16–17

hamster charm 20
hamster facts 30
handling your hamster 7
hay feeder 13
hideaways 12, 13

"keep out" sign 19
key ring 9

lantern 14–15

maze 22–3

nocturnal animals 7, 14, 30
notecards 11, 21

paints 5, 17
paper crafts 10–11
paperweight 18
party 26–9

pencil pot 24–25
pencil topper 9
pet record book 10
piñata 28–29
pocket hamster 6–7
poster paints 17

recycling 22–25

safety 5, 16, 17, 23, 26
salad bar 16–17
salt dough 20

tea lights 15
templates 31
terracotta pots 17
treats 13, 16–17, 23, 26, 29

wild hamsters 13
woven pot 24–25